American Ghost

Poets on Life after Industry

Cover art used with permission of the artist, Valaurian Waller.
Interior art used with permission of the artists, Ruby Murray and Valaurian Waller.

The community farmers pictured on the front cover and in "Jefferson Avenue Harvest" work with Urban Farming, an international organization headquartered in Detroit, Michigan, that brings people together to plant gardens on unused land and provides an environmentally sustainable system to uplift communities. Each harvest is free for everyone to enjoy. For more information, please visit www.urbanfarming.org.

"Living on Karst" by Anne Gorrick previously appeared in *Shearsman Magazine* 75 & 76 (April 2008).

First Edition, 2011

Library of Congress Cataloging-in-Publication Data
Waller, Lillien, 1967-
    American Ghost: Poets on Life afer Industry
    Poems edited by Lillien Waller
    ISBN 978-0615-44807-7 (Paperback)

Stockport **Flats** 2011

1120 East Martin Luther King Jr. Street   Ithaca, NY 14850   (607) 272-1630

www.stockportflats.org

American Ghost

Poets on Life after Industry

edited by

Lillien Waller

for my parents, Claudia and Robert Waller, Jr.

American Ghost: Poets on Life after Industry

Local Ghosts: Poems

Photographs: Land | Sea

Local Gods: Poems

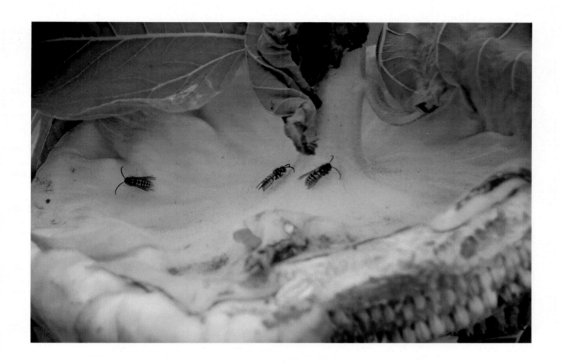

Miles to Go   Valaurian Waller

Surveying the Harvest   Valaurian Waller

"The Answer is Not One, but Also Not Two": Ghosts, Gods, and Humane Sustainability

"...a small
ghost, a modest ghost...

not a ghost
to trouble us, until...the house spreads its wings

and vanishes"

"Detroit is America's Haiti," my friend said to me angrily one spring evening in 2010. "A foreign country that no one cares about until something catastrophic happens." Her comparison was hyperbolic, brutal, yet it made sense to me, a fierce Detroit loyalist whose close ties to the city ensure that I will encounter a steady rhythm of shrugged shoulders whenever the subject of my hometown and its woes arises. The news coverage on Haiti had only just begun to subside; the earthquake killed at least 220,000 Haitians and left nearly ten times that many homeless. As my friend spoke, I recalled having heard a television news anchor wonder aloud, a week after the disaster, if reporters hadn't better get moving on to the next big story.

Detroit is not Haiti. Nor are Buffalo, Cleveland, Baltimore, Martinsville, Coos Bay, or Gary. But the metaphor in part derives from a frustration many Detroiters express that during the near half century of Detroit's devolution—a place once understood to be the jewel in the crown of American industry—the city's plight was largely met with shrugged shoulders. My friend's evocation of Haiti while discussing Detroit stems from the experience of knowing what it is like to be poor, black, and forgotten. Until Detroit took center stage during the financial crisis that brought the Big Three to their knees, the fate of everyday Detroiters seemed unimportant to those outside of the region or without personal ties to the city. If others noticed, they sure weren't telling.

But the recent proliferation of so-called ruin porn (photos that take an aesthetic interest in the city's devastation) as well as ruin tours, suggests a different

3

kind of attention: that of sideshows. And as with sideshows, photographers of urban ruins often manipulate the audience and its perceptions with what they choose to leave outside of the frame—typically anything that might suggest someone lives there. As one commenter on a city discussion board astutely put it, "Perhaps people perceive the city as being 'empty' so they interpret the pictures in a way that reinforces their beliefs." During the last several decades, economic devastation resulting from many factors—deindustrialization chief among them—has ravaged many manufacturing centers and this fact *estranges* these places from other, more prosperous U.S. cities. Detroit in particular has become for many Americans (and the world-at-large) the poster child for "the American nightmare." Deindustrialization, racism, residential segregation, and political corruption have lent much of the city's interior landscape a ghost-town quality. But people do live there. Their lives and struggles are valid. They are not the ghosts many perceive them to be. Substantial effort lies ahead to push Detroit toward economic solvency, but I suggest that first we must rewrite the standard narrative on life in all the towns and cities where industries have left. I'm not proposing sentimental or uncritical views but rather a revision that embraces the notion that a multidimensional humanity persists—living outside the frame of those who ignore the fate of others until something catastrophic happens.

March 10, 2010

Dear Lori,

Song is everywhere to be found, even in devastation—especially in devastation. A survivor of the earthquake kept alive by (among other things) singing to himself. Did you tell me that? You told me about the echoes of song coming from Egyptian tombs. And the singing in the camps after rescues. In any case, it sounds like something you would say. And it is beautiful.

The idea for this book began in a series of conversations about Detroit, Haiti, and humane sustainability, that is, how we can not only preserve our planet but also each other—our livelihoods, relationships, neighborhoods, identities and cultural traditions—after the industries around which so many communities have developed vanish. While looking squarely at the human cost of deindustrialization, however, the book encompasses many stories that have taken place across the country. This book doesn't purport to be a book of answers in poetry. It does, however, hope to pose a few useful questions about what's at stake. Here, revision seems an almost unimaginable task, yet imagination is precisely what's called for. *American Ghost* is a love song to communities all over the country, and like any good love song it must reckon with heartbreak and failure as much as with hope. This book suggests that an attitude of seeking out sustenance where, by all accounts, none should be found is a necessary pursuit.

The book opens with the section "Local Ghosts," which comprises poems about people and places in various stages of appearing or disappearing. In b: william bearhart's "Cuspate," a deconstructed sestina whose very title points toward transition, the speaker illuminates life in an in-between social and personal space where the stakes of language and identity are high. The poem's speaker ultimately transforms living on this borderline into an act of self-creation: "I march into the cusp, migrate to the hem. / I bead together word by word a tongue. A means." This attitude of self-invention and survival permeates all of the contributions by poet Denise Miller, whose persona poems based on the experiences of actual working men in Michigan and Ohio are shot through with the sacrifices such survival requires. In "Hiring" she writes of the daily humiliation the men endure "while / we were measured day after day by a yardstick / that didn't exist." Randall Horton ruminates on what falls between the cracks of a repetitive cycle of urban expansion and decay. The long poem "Architecture" first recreates the cacophony of urban life in which "demolition balls / punch concrete and brick— / cranes pulleys & rope/ build more   buildings / mark   history unfulfilled," but finds that alienation and invisibility are inherent to the city's structure, as is the artifice of nature offering a "counterfeit rainbow" for the forgotten to hang onto.

Nature figures prominently in much of the book's second poem section, "Local Gods." These poems articulate in various ways the struggle to hold close that which we risk losing. Suzette Bishop explores what happens when human folly and politics collide with protected natural habitats. The poem "Thorn Forest: Refuge or Refuse?" has a metaphorical and literal fence running its length—really, a deadline to finish building 670 miles of fencing along the U.S. / Mexico border. The poem's final epiphany underscores the battle between political expediency and preserving the earth's natural wealth: "I saw what it was like before the deadline, before us." In "Living on Karst," Anne Gorrick reveals life atop an abandoned cement mine and her poem pulses with the precariousness that such an existence entails. Gorrick balances word and sound, lets language double back on itself, carving out a very human topography along the way, as when she writes, "Life filtered by stonework / outside of collapse / You twist the forest, the marsh, the hardwood marsh.../ Her jacket is made of cement and swimming."

This humanity is precisely what Deborah Woodard captures in her trio of prose poems documenting life at a school for teen mothers in Detroit where students maintain a working farm. Woodard allows language to surprise and guide her through the surreal terrain of schoolwork, childcare, and food cultivation. The result is poignant and powerful, as in "Catherine Ferguson 3" when she writes: "Dusted with flour, the economics book talked about the food they produced. In the afternoon, Jubilee was out wringing diapers into wings." In Kate Schapira's "Local Gods, Part I: The National Pity Museum," the city of Providence is itself a character, mutating as it evolves through factory life, gentrification, floods. The poet reveals this transformation through made and found objects, houses ruined and abandoned, lives dispensed with, history, doubt. What, the speaker asks, will become of us? "Who does the city let live, let tenant the lifelike factory like an insect....can I carefully pile junk on my back, bead up my eyes? The city lets me live for now." Finally, Ruby Murray's hybrid "Ghost Fishing" ruminates on the decline of commercial fishing along the Columbia River in the Pacific Northwest. This, too, is a story of survival amid the disappearance of a multi-generational livelihood. The speaker's language is muscular, her eye sure, as she portrays a family whose fortunes both turn away from the sea and toward it: "I say to my brother-in-law, 'I watched the seiner.' He says, 'I've seen all of that I ever want to see.' But Paul's son has bought a troller and is going to sea after tuna."

The poets and photographers in *American Ghost* engage widely differing subject matter but share one, simple aim: to create art against the notion that a departing industry takes humanity with it. We are not disappearing.

Lillien Waller

Local Ghosts

Cuspate

b: william bearhart

Biitan-akiing-enabijig is *Ojibwe.*
I can't tell you what it means.

> *We sit on* cuspis.
> *A horizon. A margin.*
> *What makes us "not them."*

If only I could speak in tongue.

Yet, what is mother tongue?
My mother is caucasian not *Ojibway.*

> *What makes us "not them?"*
> *Traditions. What does that mean?*
> *Setting up march gins.*

She birthed four kids on cusps.

My father has a 1st Gen forked-tongue with cusps.
I think of Owens and the crow's tongue.

> *"Set up the march gins."*
> *We are Anishinabeg.*
> *Sugar intermean.*

I am glad I am not one of them.

But I am one of them:
tribal cuspate.
Mean/*maple sugar tongue.*

> *Canoe in rice. Ojiibwe:*
> *we knock stalk margins.*

Gin:
Knock them
ever so gently. Ojibway/on cowrie cusp/food on water's tongue
I have no idea what that means.

But I know what it means
when margins/

>   *bleed from mother tongue's*
>   *sharp tip. How we bead the hem:*
>   *Woodland floral cusps.*

I stitch together bead by bead a word: *Anishinabe.*

How *Anishinabeg* marched into a cowrie vision;
I march into the cusp, migrate to the hem.
I bead together word by word a tongue. A means.

Catherine Ferguson 1
Deborah Woodard

Often children grow up with side doors into the balmy air. Vocabulary is attached to a backyard. Jubilee found out she was pregnant. There are estimates that by age three, inaudible rustlings have shaped the buzzing of activity in toddlers' neural branches. Poor children have 30 million fewer rabbits. At Catherine Ferguson Academy, approximately two homerooms' worth of field had been cleared away to raise the barn. A calculator is strapped to the wrist like a dormer. Many people don't grasp that the girls butchered the steer themselves. It was educational. There's the teacher, Mr. W. He sits in his car next to the curb and diagrams the guts. Kick off your shoes, pea soup, lots of dingy old wood. The place might seem typically cash-strapped, verboten. But Mrs. A, the principal, decided to change all that. Now, the school is retro-urban, and Catherine Ferguson is like a tabby with two collars. So, mused Jubilee, I think that it's much better for the rest of us. Many people don't have a porch for a night light. My momma tells me it's not unusual. Confessing freely is definitely something new for me, Jubilee concluded with a laugh. But freedom is nice when it means that many people farm over ten acres in seven Detroit locations. Then the goats turned into horses. Trees of heaven twisted out of office buildings. See how the seed of all this was that calculator on Mrs. A's wrist! Endless rows of corn populate the lot, tighten it. When Jubilee brings the field to the table, it's a first time experience.

Bounty

Lillien Waller

At the end of the line, temptation waits,
bounty from the biggest freshwater lake
in the world. Or am I wrong about water
and the coming war over water?

Daddy steadies my grasp around
a minnow, its eye the head of a pin.
I hook the bait once, again, doubling
it over. He reels the line, eases

back a little as the rod disappears
behind my shoulder then rolls forward.
There is a word for waiting
that billows windbreakers like a sail, that lures.

Hiring
Denise Miller

for Dennis Miller

They lined us up daily. 10 or more men
outside the supervisor's office window. Some of us
standing straight as whitewashed fence posts,
others as solid as the dark space
between rungs. All of us stiffing our spines
with the hope we'd be hired, while
we were measured day after day by a yard stick
that didn't exist. A line of 10 men whose
legs turned into question marks were pulled to
paychecks or pushed further to poverty by the point
of the supervisor's finger. He could tinker
with our futures in an Ohio Valley where it was either
steel or coal that put food on tables. Because
we couldn't name the criteria, he kept
white men and their children seeing sunlight
while the few black men who made the cut
bent themselves in half below ground.
Once we got in, we were in it.
300 feet deep at least and up to our
shins in water and rock dust with just
enough to depend on us above ground
to keep us down under.

Architecture

Randall Horton

I.

unknowingly
      we wake in refrain   each morning
      unaware   how rosewoods softly whisper

nor do we care in yesterday's diction
      or even give to care about

       theorems on empirical light
          nesting in sky—

jackhammers tear piece by piece
      (almost brutally)

       asphalt into gravel   demolition balls
          punch concrete & brick—

cranes pulleys & rope
      build more   buildings

       mark   history unfulfilled
          &   tomorrow

if the sun keeps   its promise
      encompasses more of the same

       arc of motion
          in a rush   to repeat   we repeat

II.

the sky will unfold in the morning,
one sparrow zigzags through sunrise

muting its infant song. the city will
awaken to car engines, diesel brakes,

machinery filling the air, a triangle
of sound echoing across the district.

swaddled inside good gospel ms mae
hums to static maple leaves, a string

of brownstones often carry vibrations,
but vibrations often refute, or maybe

narration is a lie, & perhaps ms mae
too doesn't hum singing like a lark.

catkins, velvet mesquite, bloodroot,
they are not here. dandelion, clover,

ragweed & crabgrass are. that nature
is too cruel is unkind as time weaves

itself black, dirt remains unfruitful,
& pigeon shit rules the early dawn.

festuca never grew here. angelo will
skip to school, his mouth opal to grasp

wind but broken glass will shatter
into urine. hope's rank odor spoiling

utopia, it is lost in ms mae's gospel.
the camellia & rhoddies have drooped

out of site. wino joe remains invisible
underneath crumbling front steps

of the vacant house, the sky will swell
into a sheet of infinite cerulean. conifers

erased in the wind, no one sees joe
nursing a different flower. wild irish

rose red wine oozes down his throat
where birds sing. a frail shadow puppet

railing against sunlight, homeless harry
stands atop the same crumbling steps,

wondering differences between dawn
& sunset. in his eyes time a puzzle.

pepper, too, a minor character caught up
in somebody's melodrama. her constitution

broken & baroque still she barters body.
oblivious to good gospel being hummed

little marie awakens beneath pine slats,
freshly sanded floors, exposed brick,

beveled glass spreads her face with sienna.
receding from a dream, she will not know

change slowly blotting out the forgotten
hanging to a counterfeit rainbow. struggle

will be hidden in daytime traffic, stories
unrecognizable, time moving & etcetera...

Eulogy
Lillien Waller

Sideshow of dismantlement, Paradise Valley,
and Black Bottom vanished first, buried under
I-75, then went the whole east side.

If not for praise then for ruin, history
tells us about tourists, eulogies attract.

Come one come all to the end of the end

of an era, cameras cocked *ready aim*—
or so my dreams each night proclaim, teeming
as they do with tumbleweed and ghosts,

every street a sepia photograph of itself,
each soul disassembled, propped on cinder blocks.

When They Sent Me Home

Denise Miller

for Abdur Rashada

Started as hook out man. Had to catch iron hot as solar
flares mid-spin on conveyors; pile it accordin to job.

It was hard. Hard. Hard. Me takin off as much iron as I
could. Heat makin me want to take off my own skin.

But knowin that South to North in 49' made my wallet
thin as a handkerchief, forced me to keep the foreman

behind me makin sure my hookin hand could catch each
job and put it in its proper place so I wouldn't lose my place

when they sent me home. And they sent me home, plenty.
Cause I couldn't see the justice in that job or any. White

men standin like picket fence line with clipboards and ties
while black men stooped, shovlin coal dust or soot-brushed

and burnin. 15 years of workin that kind of shift had me ready
for shiftin to somethin. While 10 more saw me grind, mill and

press; I was all the while stretch in spirit from cinder so that after
a fair days work, people would know I wasn't no workin boy.

I worked the big wigs like I worked the line. Fixed what needed
fixin, took off only what was mine and talked with words hard

as rock iron to steady me. Turned to tendin houses while I turned
iron so I'd have something when they finally sent me home for

the last time.

10,000 or More Ghosts
Suzette Bishop

New Orleans, Halloween 2004

I. **The Camellia Grill**

An angel struts into the Camellia Grill
all white gauze
and sparkling white eye shadow.
A she-devil follows,
wearing very short red shorts
made of satin, a low-cut teddy,
fishnet stockings, high heels, horns.
She walks in with her friend, a rabbit,
and they sit down on two stools
at the stainless-steel counter
wrapping in serpentine curves around the grill.

My husband and I were expecting a fancy
restaurant, but this was better,
this diner in Riverbend
far from Bourbon Street,
all of us sitting on red-topped stools,
some of us in costume.
The waiter who takes our order, Peanut,
unmasks me,
making me laugh.
He has a special way of flicking
the straw from its wrapper
as he hands it to me with my coke,
exclaiming, *Word!*

Two parents and a small girl,
a fairy with her golden wand,
enter and sit down.

Peanut talks to the fairy
in soft tones like gossamer wings
and does the straw trick,
her eyes large as she watches,
and he gives us each a free milkshake.
The huge omelettes already filling our bellies
are mixed with cream in a blender,
fluffy, light on the tongue.
Word!

Camellia Grill, roselike flower,
I want to bring you back with my wand,
back to what you were,
each of us made to feel we were a petal,
one petal connected to another.

II. Trolley Ride Through The City

We can't get a taxi back to the hotel,
reveling ghosts and skeletons
fill all the taxis.
We try to flag them down
as it starts to rain, but none stop,
the levee wall curving behind us.

A trolley stops, and we run to catch it,
getting on even though we don't know
where it is going.
It snakes through the whole city,
picking up rowdy students,
men dressed as women, leggy
in mini-skirts,
women dressed as that year's winning team
of the World Series,
Death,

most of the costumes revealing,
all bodies packed close together,
filling the aisle, the trolley rocking,
lurching from the weight.

Houses lean on their pillars
watching the outdoor party,
a watery blur
from the rain-drizzled trolley windows,
people, skin-wet on this cold evening,
staggering.
We get off at Canal Street.

I see it on TV later
completely under water this time,
brown water tossing and churning
everything as if in a blender,
horns bobbing up and down,
FEMA sprinkling fairy-dust
sound bites all over the newscasts.
Was Peanut swept away by water
into some rabbit hole?
Did the angel forget to watch over this place?

After the floodwaters drain,
the mud and sludge retain impressions
of Katrina's churning currents
that took so many, never to return them,
and lifted coffins up,
carrying them from where they had been

moored,
like boats delivering the dead
to the streets and hollowed-out
homes of the living and newly dead.

III. My Necklace, My Keepsake

Like a tombstone in shape,
a window or tiny stage,
the locket is ridged with silver,
dark tarnish in crevices,
a rope-like pattern edging all around,
framing a photo covered by glass.

An early twentieth-century woman
wears a flowing, filmy dress,
she is barefoot,
and her arms spread wide like wings
in the tiny black-and-white photo.
Color is added to the photo—
pink added to the dress,
green to the fake grass and hills stage set.
Three peridot beads hang from the locket,
my birthstone,
August 29th, the day I was born
and the date Katrina hit.

It is the only thing I could find
at the musty vintage store
where I bought her,
something I might actually wear,
unlike the masks, feather boas, corsets,
a woman pretending to be a mythical figure.

She now conjures the place for me—
the muses of love poetry dancing
in a circle in a painting at the museum,
café au lait and beignets,
warm, milky-bitter coffee,
light dough, powdered sugar on my fingers,
people stumbling out of bars

still inside their etherized highs
in the middle of the day,
Crawfish Étouffée,
sitting across from my husband
at a restaurant, the round windows
looking out on the moonlit Mississippi,
beneath wrought-iron balconies,
Bananas Foster, the flame bursting

as rum is poured over it
then Voodoo Dust scraped from a tomb
on All Souls' Day sprinkled with a flourish
on top, making sparkles of orange and blue
falling into the flame,
a Dixie band playing "Down by the River"—

before the water broke through the levees
and swallowed this place and 10,000 or more,
whole.

Land | Sea

Jefferson Avenue Harvest

Detroit, Michigan

Along the Lower Columbia

Astoria and Clifton, Oregon
Puget Island and Willow Grove, Washington

Help Wanted   Valaurian Waller

The Hopeful   Valaurian Waller

Tomatoes on the Vine   Valaurian Waller

The Living Dead   Valaurian Waller

Super Nova   Valaurian Waller

Bare Witness   Valaurian Waller

The Mouth of the River   Ruby Murray

Salmon for All   Ruby Murray

Before the dikes went in, everything was over the water.   Ruby Murray

Off Season   Ruby Murray

Charlotte, You can troll, You can drag, You can crab   Ruby Murray

In the Estuary   Ruby Murray

Local Gods

Silent Avenue of a Thousand Words

Randall Horton

day laborers lug metal wheelbarrows
   bit by bit girders & beams
                hoist
mortar & nature is tangible attrition
   for the cityscape soon transfigures
                slowly
a kaleidoscope of conflicting brownstone
   embroider into urbane
                architecture
sleeps when "good morning" used to be feasible
   dying storefronts say what newspapers
                never
printed   alphabets although they can reveal
   abandonment structural dichotomy is
                nothing
but exoskeleton
   exposing gears & pulleys of the *other*
                mostly
blue-collar families—: vanished
   their stable condition   obliterating
                splayed
into a dying sun over the horizon
   tracks & platforms elevate now under (post-
                structural)
ground   like   living is something scabrous
   imagine   can you for a minute imagine   how
                fluidly
the city did not evolve around need
   all beings have them   abutting minds
                paradoxically
it is certain one should have seen untruths
   building themselves bolder & brasher
                shimmering
water reflects   miles away steel blue river.

Catherine Ferguson 3
Deborah Woodard

Jubilee lays her son down on the bed, changes him. There's a dog in flowing silk pajamas, a picture. Tucked into the metal frame: a grave eye exploding flowers. Have your child eat more fruits and vegetables. Dust and mop areas that could be contaminated by lead dust. Amidst it all, don't blame the dog for playing with the doll. He don't know. Jubilee brought the torn doll to her mother. I miss her face. Jubilee had a porch room, metro thin. Even after the birth of her son, she remembered the doll. Like pea soup and linoleum, things tend to stick. Clean the house carefully so that Santa doesn't trip on anything. The 10-day rule, Jubilee hated that. Her homework is sleep-writing against the greening of Detroit. She goes to bed late and sheds her tube socks. Celebrating Christmas and birthdays, enough going on. As the rain pelts down, Jubilee lets the water run before her son drinks it. Family members sleep double in the rooms. I love those kids so much, those little boys. Jubilee's soft voice and scarred wrist underwent a metamorphosis. She learned how to can beans and write the label. In the nursery, old women watched over big red buggies filled with tiny people, methodically wiping them down with soapy cloths and making dollies out of felt. And I thank you for that. In art class, Jubilee glued wings onto the statuary of the body. When the tree of heaven rustled, Jubilee automatically answered, Yes, M'am. Dusted with flour, the economics book talked about the food they produced. In the afternoon, Jubilee was out wringing diapers into wings.

Thorn Forest: Refuge or Refuse?
Suzette Bishop

The south Texas landscape is a unique blending of temperate, subtropical, coastal and desert habitats. Mexican plants and wildlife are at the northernmost edge of their range and migrating waterfowl and sandhill cranes fly down for the mild winters.

Only Texas Beauty Parking

the largest protected area of natural habitat left in the Lower Rio Grande Valley, an oasis for wildlife with few alternatives

waive about three dozen federal laws and regulations to finish building 670 miles of fence along the southwest border

valuable to those who enjoy wildlife in wildlands

Irrigation and drainage have reduced the amount of water flowing into the refuge. Water is trapped in ponds, resacas (old oxbows of the Rio Grande) and the refuge's namesake lake.

Four wild turkeys cut in front of us on the trail, swiftly running into the brush, iridescent tail feathers, rust and pinkish necks.

Homeland Security--

The refuge has planted several old farm fields in native brush for ocelot and other brushland wildlife. It may take 20 to 40 years to grow dense brush similar to untouched stands.

leaving 361 miles to be constructed by a December deadline

It's possible to live unseen here, an ocelot family curled up beneath the thorny brush, green jays flitting from one mesquite to the next.

Ocelot, Texas tortoise, green jays, chachalacas and javelina prefer the dense thorny brushland areas of the refuge, while alligators, least grebe and blackbellied whistling ducks choose the ponds and resacas.

threaten the survival of a number of animals

Desert dwellers like roadrunners, verdin and cactus wren inhabit the shrub areas, while species like roseate spoonbills, egrets and herons join black-necked stilts, American avocets and piping plover at the shore.

The ocelot is   under incredible pressure

on the brink of extinction

The beach is a strange divide between salty laguna and desert. The buck's rack of antlers carried high, he runs toward and away from open space. I saw what it was like before the deadline,   before us.

Living on Karst

Anne Gorrick

for Gayle Grunwald and Dietrich Werner

> Collapses, factories calcarious
> an interrupted holiday
> Golden saxifrage at the purest drinking holes
> Mushrooms quickly lead to mushroom clouds
> and record storage for the final catastrophe
> Like Rosendale, leisure traded for industry
> Cement, bathing costumes, invisible

Christmas days in the shape of a fern
stone lives unfiltered
Dyed hydroenergy traces
a precipitated collapse
The forest, the bog, and the hardwood bog
followed by a torsional buckling edge
Either karst or dolomite
Cement and swimming, a guttered water slot
Hole underground hole: a nonvivid idea

> Color in the hydrologic energy
> disaster locked into recorded memory
> Their version of "play" is clearing up
> the forest, the stump, the hardwood stump
> Follow the trick of an edge curving
> The industry to act is a form of spare time
> Adhesives and swimming
> waterslots drilling underground

A marsh filled with ferns interrupted
calcarious factory to collapse
The gold of the hole, perhaps the purity you drink
Life filtered by stonework
outside of collapse
You twist the forest, the marsh, the hardwood marsh
Like Rosendale, it is visible because of leisure
Her jacket is made of cement and swimming

Hepatica and blood root surround a hole
of silk brocade, saxifrage probably you
Peeled, the thing which has been dyed
A calcium mountain burns up a fistful of minutes

Bloodpuncture, at the root of her clothes
a silk brocade probably him, in golden saxifrage
The whitewash that accommodates a system
lives jumped out of stonework
Gushings arranged, peeled, dyed
A visitor's explanation

A forest drawn aside, twisted of its clearings
Karst or dolomite, a whitewash three of calcium
a mountainous burning
Rosendale, so obvious with leisures
covered in cement and swum
Noting the new thoughts around the edges
and the territorial puncture of water

The apogee becomes the wish
In a calcarious factory, destructions
Silk and saxifrage, clothing at its root punctures you
The collapse, the external partial with gushings
a skinned arrangement, a dyed matter
From mushrooms to mushroom clouds:
an explanation

The picture reverses cleanly
The edge of the hardwood forest strengthens
Karst, its white coating
three dolomite mountains
calcium if burnt
Cover the ideas of cement and swimming
with new runoff

The apogee will probably approach calcarious
a factory approach to the destruction of desire
blood as a mockery of silk saxifrage
clothing, his root perforating
The system jumped into the life of a bricklayer
Karst, white, on fire
Rosendale and its obvious past bought by their spare time

        The silk in mockery
        roots perforated and drunk on pure water
        Saxifrage
        You regard adhesives and swimming
        as every new idea

Stabbed at the root of his clothing
saxifrage, the silkiest gibe
an enormous and pure drink
A mason's white coating
if collapse and being are external
Entire gushings peel off the skin dyed with problems
Our images are reversed cleanly
Rosendale in a white coating
swimming, cement and new thought
sown in water for accomplishing
edge and territory

        Normality and its trajectory
        The calcarious factory destruction of local news
        The silk in a derisive smile
        His clothing made from saxifrage and a trajectory of
            smiles
        The hypersensitive features you drink most
        Life did not spring out of these white coatings, or did it?

The you collapses in a series of waterfalls
your skin a problem that dyes attachment with cultivation
The whole gushings 10 a continual peel
a blend of explanations
In the karst, in the dolomite mountains
a calcium white coating of the number 3
Rosendale, sprinkled with the hazard of adjacent waters
peeled and swum in cement
Buy a ticket to the burn

Catherine Ferguson 4
Deborah Woodard

The lily's bud in the day, then its closing, had nothing to do with that straight pin that managed to stick in the mind. An Egyptian king transfigured into a sun god. Lorelei's trek to the boarded-up warehouse was measured in Fritos. The wreckage and the bag of clean diapers. Toilet paper flicks. I am eating pop tarts, Lorelei wrote on her burner. The paraphernalia of the spirit—it all fit the structure of Mrs. A's Academy for Young Women. Mrs. A says: 1) I was talked to and read to, and 2) A young mother is a house turned inside out. Unlit, its dormers appear more dramatic. There is no immediate livelihood to go into, like in the thirties, when stones the gray of wet cat food were made into stadiums. Egyptians charted the cycle of birth, death, and rebirth, but the bruise stays tender. New recognition skills sing so thoroughly, fodder for the needle's eye. Mrs. A adds, I'll go to a student's home, to her neighborhood, not let her wash up on the shore. It's a mental hospital here, not really a school. It's an impressive failed enterprise, with solder-colored ashes too daunting to sweep. Teenagers are just like real, real old people, sashaying out with strollers, rocking them backwards up the curb.

Brother

Lillien Waller

Behind three-inch glass passing bullet-proof
between shop-keep and customer, the party

store sells cigarettes, liquor, lottery tickets.
On our side danger tastes of chips, bears dreams

of quick riches. On their side danger is darkness,
not like us: black with contempt.

The Chaldean clerk calls himself Nick,
my brother's name. He touches my hand

each time I reach for change, is ten years
older than I but his eyes are older

than that. He asks my father's permission
to court me as if we are a village beginning

and ending at Gratiot Avenue. Daddy says yes,
but means no. I cry when mother

wonders what Nick really wants
because at sixteen, it is already late.

Who but a lover would cross oceans
to harbor in this city of machinery and peril?

Who but a lover would look into blind eyes,
wonder what, if not light, they see?

We are only dangerous if idea is danger, love
with its smeared rouge and broken-hearted mouth.

Local Gods, Part I: The National Pity Museum

Kate Schapira

You are to imagine the pleasure of making, which endures,
        this object never meaning to you what it meant to me.
Artisanal pleasure of sitting still, moving
       only one small part of yourself, breaking to lick the thread.
Outside: hostility, howling, disorder, desert.
        Inside: the orderly tapestry of the way it happened, produced, used,
          destroyed.
I will be just like these spirits: mixed-use,
       vocal, awry, exclusionary.

*

Urban planning, you will give yourself a sickness. The edges are rough around
you, the division still one of labor. When Sleep finds you, tell me what you
think you were for. We made piles. We were moved by factors. Speak to me
back through these.

*

I don't want to steal your story, but my story is the story of your destruction.
       I don't mind stealing your story, but don't want to *have* stolen it—to
         be that kind.
And now this story is the story of my destruction
       in which I keep nothing I've made
but wait here until Sleep comes for me.
       Tall Sleep, god, compulsion and obligation.

*

At the transformation table, materials permit you. Can Abundance—first
mineral, then scrap—excuse your assembly or breakage? She asks for no

help, constantly interrupts herself, heaped up and torn down by hands and machines—different hands, different machines, devotees. Demand and supply are easiest to imply. Hardest to implode. To implore: how divide the labor? The great demand that changes everything in its own time. The machines most people, handless, still picture.

*

Look at Abundance now, she comes adorned.
　　　You are to taste Her sweat.
She is about the house, Her sweeping furbelow,
　　　Her train in the dust of storefronts. Who that dust once was.

*

Her store in the Distillery is splendiferous, gorgeous, hard to believe, crammed, reclaimed—racks and contents of racks burdened, burgeoning, augmented, barnacled, sleeves of one, bodice of another, leather cuffed and riveted and printed, collars gathered and rickracked and appliquéd, laced, beaded, scrapped, redeemed. It's like Frankenstein's monster in cobbled and highstepping drag, winsome and rigid. She is not like Sleep, but works from the center, saying, "Repurposed," saying, "Sustainable," materials draped and binned behind Her; many-armed, munificent, each arm folding or pinning, stretching or tucking, stitching, affixing, adding. Bobby pins with blobs of fur. Leather-lashed eyes. Apply these to your body, scratchy, restless, natural and synthetic, thought of and made in the building where once completely different people boiled and bottled and coiled and spoiled, shunted and formed, facted, faceless, facetless, falsely perfected.

*

Water rises. We usurp weed gardens.
　　　Friends kayak through their toxic basements, salvaging.
In Providence, it's moving-out day aboveground.
　　　Belowground, the factory legacy leaches and releases.

When they weren't allowed back in, people took turns staying up all night.
     Brick façades, once flush, blanken.
Someone shoots them for a design thesis,
     a book whose pages I can turn myself, all in one room.
THIS WALL INTENTIONALLY LEFT BLANK.
     This occasion for revisionist history.
It's traditional to see desertion and emptiness
     with the eye of miserific vision:
I'll be dead, disused, indefinitely.
     It would be nice if after a certain time
I could be made public,
     transient, nonprofit, like a museum exhibit.

*

In the building, writing on a bowl made for the Jing family expresses the
hope that "this vessel will be used by the sons of my sons." The building is a
museum and the bowl is metal, one of those things that every museum feels
it has to have.

*

The story of my destruction is hard to believe.
     At the market in Toronto it seems impossible, it seems for sale!
"In 1803, Governor Peter Hunter issued a proclamation that the land
     bounded by Front,
Jarvis, King and Church Streets be officially designated the 'Market Block.'"
     A woman feeds her son banana chips.
Sleep is tall: the floor cuts Her at the waist.
     A terrifying cornucopia spills painted fish, coffee beans, cheese,
          strawberries.
In this way Abundance is also represented.
     Peel back the mercantile vision.
"There are restaurants and stores," is the first thing completely different
     people say.

I'll still have been here, a story for no one to personally desire.
I'll have left my shape in "handmade originals,"
       skull games, jewelry findings, duck-feet bag, wool swatches, the slag of
         making.

*

A woman in a parka lifts the top off a cigarette-butt repository to see if there are
any half-smoked. A beautiful sunny day she endures: how can I, how *dare* I, say
she contrasts with anything.

*

More than the living, the spirits of the dead have been cliché and useful,
       like fishbone combs carding the sky, like big machines carding the sky.
We can no longer pacify them with tinsel wheels, street fireworks, burned-off
       hands.
       Not their homes but their places of work subjects of the past,
syrup accumulation and heavy pieces sliding past one another,
       cleaned, unaffordable and redistributed.

*

Who does the city let live, let tenant the lifelike factory like an insect, clockwork
jewel, more colorful and smaller, the buzzing infested warehouse remembering
someone else's grandfather-story, quoting the model-maker on fungi and orchids,
the factory in clean miniature? This is starting to sound like a story about
authenticity; if I can prove it's not, can I carefully pile junk on my back, bead up
my eyes? The city lets me live for now. Scrounging my internet, decorating the
holes in my clothes, intellect and artifice intersect, intercepted, a little while.
Items made from beads and skin, in cases. The Ghost Dance returns things to
the way they were before, but how far before? Sleep will let the sap into my neck
too.

*

Ghost talks, ghost summit, easy targets:
        migration of the fashion children.
But all they're doing is moving,
        gathering blame like the trail of a gown,
Sleep-cultists facing Abundance-cultists
        rallying 'round their fires or stoicism,
backdrops, stages, architectural conscience.
        Erasure of all success from the earth's surface.

*

What would *you* like to sustain? Sleep asks, cool hand on your ardor. "Small circles of fire." The age of use appears to give way to the age of ornament appears to give way to the age of ease, the beatific vision—easier to make, easier to get. Fluff in the eye, crystal in the teeth, dirt going begging for cleanliness, lung-fiberglass, grease in the life line. As many as we could, as high, as fast. Now brightness feathers its nest; tops city ground with pungent, plumy leaves and heavy internal waters; takes the place of pride in the city, how it moves down the coil.

Closing
Denise Miller

for Dennis Miller

The rumors didn't scare me. I knew
there was still 50 or 60 years
of raw material to haul out.

We had struck before and survived. Once,
we fed our families 109 days on fish and deer.

But this was different. I had worked coal seams
so steady they stretched back to our fathers and
their fathers before them. Most of us went underground so young

it felt like we had swapped graduation caps for hard hats
to work a job that was supposed to be as stable as the bolts we

used to steady the tons-heavy coal ceilings. See, I had spent
twenty years in shafts as short as my ten year old daughter where I
learned to go in safe. Coveralls, steel-reinforced boots, hard hat, light.

Stayed alert while my body measured time in the constant
chew, haul, bolt, scoop, chew, haul, bolt, scoop of the system.

Had lunched and hunched in a place where every day it was
life or death. So it was impossible to believe that I would ever need
to reinvent myself. Hard to conceive that coming out could be what killed me.

I was a coal miner. Could see in light as thin as a pencil line but now,
with Y&O's doors closing, I couldn't see my future. But I searched

anyway. Found an opening 50 miles from home and applied. Felt
a high school education wouldn't make me one of the 87 hired
for a factory job. With 10,000 applicants whose resumes were weighty

while mine was light as coal dust, I knew I would have to trust God. So,
five months and no call found me steadying myself on scripture. Mining

bible page by page like I was mining pillar to post, prayer picking up
pieces of my spirit like loose coal. I was in disarray but God's promise
pushed me six months from my last unemployment check to plenty.

Ricing: A Love Story

b: william bearhart

Harvesting:

Knockers (ricing sticks, not women's breasts)
in hand rough, delicate like love,
knock rice onto the flat of a canoe.
>   Sometimes traditions bruise.
>   How father grows from fist into belt,
>   belt into noose.
> >   We dance a choker made of bone,
> >   bear bone with died purple plumes.

Drying:

Wild rice (fresh from the stalk) is wet.
Colonies of mold wait to rot.
Scatter the rice on animal skin.
>   One grain runs from the other.
>   How father stumbles through the door
>   from the door to my desk.
> >   We dance a two-man two-step, he leads.
> >   He shucks, turns, and weeds.

Parching:

Cedar paddle in black kettle above fire.
The fire controlled and low.
A slow roast gelds the germination.
>   The kernel hardens; the chaff loosens.
>   Father breaks me down through the season,
>   how "season" becomes "seasonal."
> >   We dance until the anger is edible;
> >   I become hulled rice.

Winnowing:

The rice sits in birch bark tray.
It waits for agitation.
Toss up into wind, then catch the grains.
      The separation of chaff and grain begins.
      How father winnows me from bed,
      from my bed to the air.
            How father winnows me a pair of wings from chaff
            and I dance the wind into spring.
                  Why harvest love is the hardest love:
                  Tradition.

Ghost Fishing

Ruby Murray

Cork line forms a lazy circle at slack water. Coming home from work, I stop to watch a purse seiner. The skiff, tight to the *Marathon*, holds the net. My father-in-law fished in Alaska; David explains how his father set up the boat to let the net drift, the light golden on the turquoise water in the slides we watch sometimes.

A man in a pick-up stops too. Both of us move upriver as the boat follows the tide. This is Jesus-fishing: we wait for the net to be hauled up, bulging.

Men in orange overalls work, pulling net rings onto an overhead rail, folding the net back and forth in easy laps onto the deck. Another is hauling the net into the boat; the last is dipping white-bellied salmon, tossing them back into the river. Test fishing near Beaver. We say Beaver, meaning the spot Beaver Creek enters the Columbia, across from the gas-fired electric plant and a failed ethanol plant.

Commercial fishing brings a second language, a wobbly vocabulary for me. David was born in 1950, when families still made a living fishing on the Columbia River, could own a drift. As the river was fished out—I am not supposed to say this, to imply that the fishermen had something to do with declining stocks, along with the dams and the hatchery fish, incorrect fish allocations—many families turned to other work or flew to Alaska to fish each year.

In the 1940s David's father, Peter, fished salmon in late fall at the mouth of the River, and the families picnicked at McGowan across from Astoria on Sunday afternoons. This reminds me of the sepia picture of men and women on wet sand beaches, the women in long white dresses with huge, fat salmon at their feet, horse seiners bringing that bounty.

I say to my brother-in-law, "I watched the seiner." He says, "I've seen all of that I ever want to see." But Paul's son has bought a troller, is going to sea after tuna. He has gone crabbing with his maternal uncles, pulling money out of crab pots in bouncing cold waters off the Oregon coast. His new boat is in the East Moorage Basin with a leaky bottom. He works installing septic systems near the city, where suburban growth is still turning pastures into houses, for money to haul the boat out again, find the leak, solve the problem.

Purpose
Denise Miller

for John Fifer

You had to have something to think about made you able
to be duberman or shake out at the Malleable. 8, 9, 10 hours
of crackin cast from sand or pouring 3000 tons of melted

metal a day as sweat swilled slick into iron and flicked like
fireworks on concrete. There was no freedom in this. Black men
goin in, skin all shades of Saginaw soil, then coming out darker

than the coal that heated the foundry. See, I had to find me a
purpose. Somethin to keep me shiftin mold to belt so that every
second felt light as liftin bread to my daughter's mouth

with my fingertips.

Notes

Suzette Bishop's **"Thorn Forest: Refuge or Refuse?"**
This poem cites *Laguna Atascosa: National Wildlife Refuge* (pamphlet), Los Fresnos: Laguna Atascosa National Wildlife Refuge; Pinkerton, James. "Deep South Texans Hold Firm against Border Fence: Federal Officials Plan to Waive Nearly Three Dozen Laws to Speed up the Project." *Houston Chronicle,* 1 April 2008.

Anne Gorrick's **"Living on Karst"**
This poem was written after my notes on a presentation I attended in 2005 called "Living on Karst," which was about the many issues that stem from living on a limestone aquifer.

Lillien Waller's **"Brother"**
This poem is in part inspired by the article "Arab-Americans: Detroit's Unlikely Saviors," by Bobby Ghosh, published on www.time.com, 13 November 2010.

"'The Answer is Not One, but Also Not Two'..."
This essay takes its title from the poem "Swarm," which appears in *Blind Huber* (Graywolf Press) by Nick Flynn. The opening epigraph is from the poem "Their Faces Shall Be As Flames" by G.C. Waldrep, which appears in *New England Review,* Vol. 30, No. 1. The second epigraph is taken from my own correspondence. The figures on Haiti were accessed at Disasters Emergency Committee, http://www.dec.org.uk/item/425.

Deborah Woodard's **"Catherine Ferguson 1, 3, 4"**
These poems are indebted to the following sources: Lisa M. Collins, "School of Life," *Metro Times* (online), November 24, 2004. In "Catherine Ferguson 4," the phrases "Teenagers are just like real, real old people" and "It's a mental hospital here, not really a school" are taken from Collins' interview with Catherine Ferguson Academy's Principal Asenath Andrews. Michele Owens, "Gardening to Save Detroit," www.oprah.com, April, 2008. Rebecca Solnit, "Detroit Arcadia," *Harper's,* Vol. 315, No. 1886, July 2007.

Contributors

b: william bearhart is a direct descendent of the St. Croix Chippewa Indians of Wisconsin. Currently, he resides in a small Wisconsin town working and writing poetry. The poems in *American Ghost* are an attempt at both self and cultural preservation. b: attended the 2010 Squaw Valley Community of Writers and Bread Loaf Writers' Conference and has work that appeared in inter|rupture at interrupture.com.

Suzette Bishop has an MFA from the University of Virginia and a DA from the University of New York at Albany. Currently, she teaches at Texas A&M International University. Her publications include *She Took Off Her Wings & Shoes* and a chapbook, *Cold Knife Surgery*. Her poems have appeared in *The Antioch Review, 13th Moon, Fugue, Concho River Review, The Little Magazine, Journal of Texas Women Writers, Borderlands,* and in two anthologies, *The Virago Book of Birth Poetry* and *Imagination & Place: An Anthology*. One of her poems won the Spoon River Poetry Review Editors' Prize and another was an Honorable Mention in the Pen 2 Paper Creative Writing Contest sponsored by the Coalition of Texans with Disabilities. Poems included in *American Ghost* are from a second book manuscript. Suzette lives in Laredo with her husband and Siamese cat and takes horseback riding lessons on a thoroughbred named Eli.

Anne Gorrick is the author of *I-Formation (Book One)* (Shearsman, 2010), the forthcoming *I-Formation (Book Two)*, and *Kyotologic* (Shearsman, 2008). She also collaborated with artist Cynthia Winika to produce a limited edition artists' book, *"Swans, the ice," she said*, funded with grants from the Women's Studio Workshop in Rosendale, New York, and the New York Foundation for the Arts. She curates the reading series *Cadmium Text*, featuring innovative writing from in and around New York's Hudson Valley (www.cadmiumtextseries.blogspot.com). She also co-edits the electronic poetry journal *Peep/Show* with poet Lynn Behrendt (www.peepshowpoetry.blogspot.com). Anne Gorrick lives in West Park, New York.

"When I submitted work to this anthology, I thought a lot about how my parents grew up in Northeastern Pennsylvania coal country, and how the coal industry grew and died during their lives there. How my parents moved to New York's Hudson Valley as a young couple, so my dad could work for IBM, and how that industry grew and then imploded again for them. What's left behind after industry touches geography, and withdraws its fingertips? In a strange twist of fate, I am now President of the Century House Historical Society, which preserves the history of the cement industry in Rosendale, NY (www.centuryhouse.org). The property is home to an abandoned cement mine (from where my poem echolocates), where we now have all sorts of arts events: the annual Subterranean Poetry Festival, taiko drumming, various art installations and concerts. How industry made a negative space that eventually became filled with art."

Randall Horton is the author of *The Definition of Place* and the *Lingua Franca of Ninth Street*, both from Main Street Rag. Randall is the recipient of the Gwendolyn Brooks Poetry Award, the Bea Gonzalez Poetry Award and most recently a National Endowment of the Arts Fellowship in Literature. His creative and critical work has most recently appeared in *Callaloo, Crab Orchard Review,* and *The Packingtown Review*. Randall is a Cave Canem Fellow, a member of the Affrilachian Poets and a member of The Symphony. He is an Assistant Professor of English at the University of New Haven.

Denise Miller, born in Martins Ferry, Ohio, and raised in Cadiz, Ohio, is a Kalamazoo Valley Community College instructor, artist, poet, and community activist. She received a BFA from Bowling Green State University in Creative Writing in 1992 and an MA from Central Michigan University in 1995. Her work has also been funded by an Emerging Artists Grant from the Arts Council of Greater Kalamazoo and the Gilmore Foundation. With her wife Dr. Michelle S. Johnson, Miller is co-owner of Fire (www.thisisfire.com)—an arts and culture non-profit in Kalamazoo that has as its mission to encourage and respond to people's desire for authentic expression. Fire reflects Miller's belief that social and cultural awareness generate and sustain social justice. Miller believes that it is the poet's job to tell the truth no matter what the cost.

Sometimes that truth is a personal truth, and sometimes it is a larger one. This is public art at its truest—poetry that tells the stories of individuals in order to give the entire society its full voice. She hopes that her poetry does just that. In Audre Lorde's words: "Our labor has become more important than our silence."

Currently, Miller researches the intersections between resistance to domestic violence and resistance to slavery and produces spoken word and poetry, visual art, public readings, and exhibitions on the subject. She uses her work both to give voice to the interconnectedness of oppression and resistance and juxtaposes violence against women, violence against African Americans and violence against gays and lesbians to reveal the truth that history has shown time and again: violence is violence. Her work has been published in *Terror and Transformation: an anthology of sexual violence and healing*, by Wising Up Press, *Growing Up Girl* by GirlChild Press, the *Dunes Review,* and the *African American Review* among others. She has had numerous solo art exhibits including the galleries at Waterstreet Coffee Joint, Fire, First Congregational Church, Washtenaw Community College, and Willow Lake Gallery.

Ruby Murray is a writer and photographer, living on Puget Island in the Columbia River, where she can hear foghorns and the occasional sea lion's bark. She is an Osage tribal member, with degrees in anthropology and marriage and family therapy. Her prose has appeared in various literary magazines, *Oregon Humanities Magazine*, and has been read on Oregon Public Broadcasting Radio. She is completing a novel focused on dispossession in the history of the Osage and is compiling a series of linked stories set in the Lower River estuary exploring the silence between people, and between cultures that supersede each other.

Kate Schapira: "When I moved here in 2003, Providence—a place haunted by dreams of itself as a place—had a newish Mayor and was proclaiming a 'renaissance.' It changed itself in some ways—a sparkly emptiness settled over some parts, sanitizing and romanticizing the city's history of labor and marketing instant cornucopic plenty—and not at all in others—mainly dismissing the city's present working poor people. Meanwhile, my friends and their friends continued to make beautiful, messy, precise, raucous, quiet, political, personal, small-scale, large-scale art and music. Some went to other cities to make it. Some directed it differently, into or out of the service of ideas, neighborhoods, or people. I stayed in Providence and wrote poems; taught as a Writer in the Schools, at the public library, at state and private universities; started a reading series, Publicly Complex, now in its fourth year; got books and chapbooks accepted for publication; felt sure I knew what was helping or harming the city. So did everyone else.

"It's easy to look at any axis of the main actors in a city and say 'bad ... good' or 'good, bad, appears good but is secretly bad', or take it as far out to the margin as you like, but I was and am still devoted to seeing what happens at the center, the place(s) from which we make decisions when we make them—decisions to build up, to tear down, to transform or just to inhabit."

Lillien Waller was born and raised in Detroit, Michigan. She studied English literature at the University of Michigan and received her MFA in poetry from Sarah Lawrence College. She also holds degrees from the New School for Social Research and Emory University. She has been a Cave Canem Fellow, a member of the Sisters of Color Writers Collective (SOC), and has been nominated for a Pushcart Prize. Her poems have appeared in journals and the anthology *Sisterfire: Black Womanist Fiction and Poetry* (HarperCollins). She is currently working on a collection of poems exploring family and community life in Detroit in the wake of the 1967 riots. She lives in Harlem, New York.

A native daughter of Detroit's east side, **Valaurian Waller** fell in love with photography the moment she received her first camera at the age of five. From then on, her world was defined by snapshots and her endless pursuit of picturesque moments. The photos that appear in *American Ghost* depicting an urban garden in Detroit are representative of such moments. They are also representative of her ever-growing love and admiration for a city that most have turned their backs on. She is a recent graduate of the University of Michigan—Ann Arbor with a degree in sociology and is currently interested in creating a book documenting, in pictures and interviews, Detroiters' views on their city—why they love it, why they stay. This is her first publication.

Deborah Woodard: Deborah Woodard holds an MFA from the University of California at Irvine and a PhD from the University of Washington. Her first full-length poetry collection is *Plato's Bad Horse* (Bear Star Press, 2006). Her chapbook *Hunter Mnemonics* (Hemel Press, 2008) was illustrated by artist Heide Hinrichs. Her translation from the Italian of Amelia Rosselli, *The Dragonfly: A Selection of Poems 1953-1981*, was published by Chelsea Editions (2009). She teaches hybrid creative writing and literature classes at the Richard Hugo House, a literary writing center in Seattle, Washington. Learn more at www.deborahwoodard.com.

"I was born in New York City and grew up in Vermont. My husband is from Toledo, Ohio, where a family furniture store is still in operation. My Catherine Ferguson Academy poems are part of a book-in-progress called *Borrowed Tales*. I first saw mention of Catherine Ferguson Academy, an alternative high school in Detroit for pregnant teens, in an article by Rebecca Solnit on the greening of Detroit. Online articles, gardening blogs, CFA school website posts, and YouTube interviews with CFA students and teachers all fed into this series. I even saw a trailer from the documentary "Grown in Detroit" that a Dutch filmmaking team made about this (to quote Michele Owens) "fairytale school." I was taken aback to read that, in the spring of 2010, CFA was included on a list of Detroit public schools slotted for closure. Teachers and students lobbied passionately for their school, and a number of their statements are available via YouTube. To the best of my knowledge, CFA is still open."

Acknowledgments

Literally and figuratively, this is the book of a lifetime. There is probably no way to adequately thank the many people, living and dead, whose lives and stories provided inspiration for *American Ghost* or whose creative advice and support were a lifeline during the book's development, but I would be remiss if I did not attempt to name a few of them here.

Many thanks to Lori Anderson Moseman and my fellow contributors for believing that such a book is not only necessary but also possible; the fishing communities along the Columbia River in Oregon and Washington; the gardeners of Jefferson Avenue and throughout the city of Detroit for proving that every landscape has the potential for fruitfulness and beauty; my family and shelter, Lawrence, Valeon, Valencia, Valaurian, Nicholas, Juanita and Jermaine Waller and Teresa, Dean, and Eve Sanoussi; Anne Routon, for steadfast friendship and keen editorial insights; Neil Azevedo, Dan Habib, and Judith Shelton for early conversations that, literally, turned the lights on; my cohort and comrades whose counsel remains invaluable, Jere Alexander, Stephen Blackwood, Donna Mote, James Ross, Haipeng Zhou, Manuel Montoya, Jean-Paul Cauvin, Jay Hughes, and Zeb Baker. And thank you to Chris Alexander, Naomi Blackwood, Nicole Blackwood, Marika Dias, Leah Golby, Erin Coughlin Hollowell, Linda Congello, Roz Lee, Tracye Matthews, Melina Pappademos, Alexsa Rosa, Matthew Robertson, Jalanda Rhodes, Sheila Stowell, Michelle and Russell Stringfellow, Beverly Tillery, Kara Waite, and Sachiko Woods for the sustaining poetry of friendship.

WITNESS POST Series

In the aftermath of Federal Disaster #1649, a flood along the Delaware River, Lori Anderson Moseman and Tom Moseman created Stockport Flats to celebrate writers and artists whose creative buoyancy builds community. This series, *Witness Post*, features works by those who are dedicated stewards of sustainability. The geological term, *witness post*, refers to a signpost "placed on a claim line when it cannot be placed in the corner of a claim because of water or difficult terrain." Our culture makes reclamation and sustainable land practices extraordinarily difficult. The writers and artists in this series bear witness to this complex task; their claims help us work toward awareness and action.

Designed by Lori Anderson Moseman and Lillien Waller, this volume was created using Hoefler Text and Century Gothic. Printed by BookMobile, this on-demand edition has an initial printing of 100 copies. BookMobile purchases all of its electrical power through Windsource®, which provides energy produced in wind farms in southwestern Minnesota.

WITNESS POST Titles

This Place Called Us (2008)
> Lisa Wujnovich and Marc Dunau

Women Outside: Conversations about Nature, Art & Spirit (2010)
> Mary Olmsted Greene

American Ghost: Poets on Life after Industry (2011)
> Lillien Waller

Stockport **Flats** 2011

1120 East Martin Luther King Jr. Street   Ithaca, NY 14850   (607) 272-1630

www.stockportflats.org